A POEM *for* A PICKLE

FUNNYBONE VERSES

Eve Merriam
A POEM for A PICKLE

FUNNYBONE VERSES

PICTURES BY

Sheila Hamanaka

Morrow Junior Books

NEW YORK

Text copyright © 1989 by Eve Merriam
Illustrations copyright © 1989 by Sheila Hamanaka
Printed in Singapore
1 2 3 4 5 6 7 8 9 10
Library of Congress Cataloging-in-Publication Data
Merriam, Eve.
A poem for a pickle : funnybone verses / Eve Merriam ; pictures by
Sheila Hamanaka.
p.   cm.
Summary: A collection of whimsical poems and word pictures about
such special things as an electrical blackout, an ice cream fountain
mountain, and a cat's eyes in the dark.
ISBN 0-688-08137-1.   ISBN 0-688-08138-X (lib. bdg.)
1. Children's poetry, American. [1. American poetry.]
I. Hamanaka, Sheila, ill.   II. Title.
PS3525.E639P64   1989
811'.54—dc19   88-22047   CIP   AC

For Maureen Hayes

E.M.

To my children, Suzy and Kiyo

S.H.

A Poem for a Pickle

Five pennies for a nickel,
a poem for a pickle.

Two nickels for a dime,
a rhyme to pass the time.

Four quarters for a one,
a couplet just for fun

      and I'll keep the change.

1, 2, 3

Three robbers trying to get rich rich rich
stole a treasure from a niche niche niche,
carried it off without a hitch hitch hitch
until they fell into a ditch ditch ditch;
then one felt a terrible twitch twitch twitch,
one felt a needle going stitch stitch stitch,
one felt a tantalizing itch itch itch,
but the night was black as pitch pitch pitch:
so they couldn't tell which was which which which.

Rover

Rover is a wonder dog,
a marvelous pup.
Other dogs roll over,
other dogs sit up.

Other dogs pull your leg
to go for a walk,
but Rover is special:
Rover can talk.

If you don't believe me,
here's the proof.
What goes over the ceiling?
Roof, says Rover,
roof, roof, roof.

If you find that isn't
proof enough,
what's the opposite of smooth?
Rough, says Rover,
rough, rough, rough.

The Nose Knows

Skunk doesn't smell
exactly like a rose.

One the nose yeses,
one the nose noes.

Skip Rope Rhyme

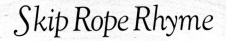

Step on a line,
step on a crack;
word from our sponsor,
be right back.

One potato, two,
three potato, four;
couch potato's nodding
more and more.

New season sitcom,
old laugh track;
prime time crime time
ack-ack-ack.

Menu

My mommy goes for veggies,
my daddy goes for meat,
I go to the ice cream store
across the street.

My mommy cuts up carrots,
my daddy chews a chop,
I make myself a sugar cone
and lick the top.

My mommy crunches celery,
my daddy dices ham,
I look in the mirror
and see how sweet I am.

Counting-out Rhyme

Granny Smith, Gravenstein,
York, Imperial,
McIntosh, Milton,
Wealthy, Rome,

Mutsu, Empire,
Stayman, Winesap,
Baldwin, Russet,
Pippin, Macoun,

Opalescent, Jonathan, Northern Spy:
Delicious in cider, sauce, or pie.

Can a Can?

A bell can ring,
a ring can be round.
Leaves can fall
in the fall
on the ground.

A watch can tell time,
you can watch the moon at night.
A pen can hold a pig,
a pen can also write.

You can punch a punching bag,
you can drink a glass of punch.
You can skip with a rope,
you can skip having lunch.

A gate can bar the way,
you can eat a chocolate bar.
If that's how peculiar
some words are—

Can a can of soup sink
to the bottom of the sink?
What do you think?

Willy-nilly

Roly-poly Hobart
and namby-pamby Nan
went out double-dating
with hoity-toity Hortense
and fuddy-duddy Dan;
they had a rowdy-dowdy pow-wow,
a razzle-dazzle time.

Specs

Four hundred and forty-four flies
fell into the apple sauce:
"This recipe calls for lots of raisins,"
said nearsighted Flossie Floss.

"This program on the teevee screen
has a very exciting waterfront scene,"
said nearsighted Angus McBean
in front of the washing machine.

Light Rain, a Downpour, and Pigeons Feasting on Crumbs from a Picnic in the Park

Pitter patter,
splitter splatter,
skitter scatter.

Crickets

Creak creak a wicker rocker
flick flick a firefly
mid-July and the creek is dryer
tick tick the time goes by.

Pick pick autumn harvest
slick slick winter ice
peek peek springtime budding
beak beak nesting birds.

Creak creak a wicker rocker
my my the old folks sigh
July again and the creek is dryer
tick tick the time goes by.

A City Ditty

Blackout in the buildings,
the big fuse blew;
no electric current,
what will we do?

Can't use the telephone,
can't make toast,
can't use the stereo,
boo, you're a ghost.

Frozen juice cans
getting runny,
frozen meat is
smelling funny.

Traffic signals out
and headlights on the cars,
but what do you know?
We can see the moon and stars.

Junk

Clank, clunk,
throw out the junk.

Here's an old sofa
with a sagging spring,
a Ping-Pong ball
without any ping,

a rocking chair
that's lost its rock,
a ticking watch
that has no tock,

a toaster that toasts
the bread too light,
a kite string that flew
away from its kite,

a pitcher for cream
with a broken lip,
a china cup
with a nice big chip.

Hunk, chunk,
throw out the junk.

If we can't get rid of one thing,
let's try another,
maybe we can give away
little baby brother.

Urban Rainbow

Pick a color
for a show:
red light stop,
green light go.

Purple neon,
orange crush,
rush-hour traffic,
hush baby hush.

Yellow sunshine
and blue for sky
when the pollution melts
by and by.

Riddle-go-round

Riddle go round and roundabout:
Is the middle of a wood
halfway in
or halfway out?

The farther in,
the nearer out?
Are you sure,
or do you doubt?

Halfway out,
or halfway in?
Guess it right
and you can win.

Haps perhaps stand your ground,
answer hasn't yet been found;
riddle go round and roundabout
and round and in and round and out.

The Ice Cream Fountain Mountain

There are so many different flavors to find,
it gets harder and harder to make up my mind,
how can I ever decide on which kind?

There's raspberry ripple,
marshmallow drip,
peppermint flagpole,
apple tooth chip;

macaroon pickle,
chocolate cheese,
pumpernickel cherry,
salami freeze;

blueberry tweed,
maple nut mink,
orange ice pizza,
raisin rum fink;

blackberry tuna,
tiddledy plum,
tomato toffee,
chrysanthemum-yum;

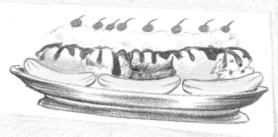

banana blubber,
French fried nectarine,
turtleneck taffy,
drip-dry tangerine;

cinnamon spasm,
pistachio burp,
cantaloupe clam,
slime of lime slurp;

nesselrode yo-yo,
butterscotch tape,
frenzy of apricot,
barefooted grape;

wheat germ parfait,
wall-to-walnut sludge,
and the special today
is frankfurter fudge.

A Rainy Day

No balls are batted,
dog's fur is matted,
crossing guard is rubber-hatted,
sidewalk is splatted,
hair curl is flatted,
quarrels are spatted,
scraggly cat is scatted,
dampness is dratted.

Queen Regina

Queen Regina
always wore
a gorgeous golden crown.

One day she forgot
to wear her ears
and the crown slipped down.

Molly's Glasses

Molly dropped her glasses
into molasses.
Icky sticky gluey goo.

She mopped up the muck
until the mop
got stuck.

Now Molly's glasses
are icky sticky gluey gooey
soppy gloppy moppy.

A New Song for Old Smoky

On top of the teevee
all covered with rust,
I found a weird item
a-turning to dust.

I asked the computer
to please take a look
at whatever the thing was
and the printout read B*O*O*K.

At Sea

To sail,
to float
adrift in a boat.

What
if it's not
a sloop
or a yacht
or liner
or schooner
or cutter
or cruiser
or ketch
or a yawl?
Haul away!

A trawler
or smaller,
a skiff or a gig,
a raft, a brig,
a kayak, a junk,
catamaran, canoe,
or dinghy
can do.

My Family Tree

BABY JUNE

Baby June
has a tune
in her head

and when it's time for bed,
she'll go just as soon
as you sing her the tune

that nobody knows
except
June.

UNCLE DICK

Uncle Dick
has a trick;

he can pick up his heels
and make them click.

Sometimes,
in the damp air,
they stick there. . . .

BROTHER PETE

Brother Pete
will eat
anything
if it's sweet.

Peppermint soup,
or ice cream on toast.

Though what he likes most
is a jelly sandwich
without any bread.

Or a bubble gum chop.
Chew your meat thoroughly, Pete.
  "I am. Cancha hear me?" *Pop!*

SISTER ANN

Sister Ann
has a Japanese fan
with a picture on it
of Ann with a Japanese fan
with a picture on it
of Ann with a Japanese fan
with a picture on it
of Ann with a Japanese fan
with a picture on it of tiny Ann
with a tiny Japanese fan
with a picture on it that's so tiny
you can only tell what it is
when you close your eyes.

A Commercial for Spring

Tired of slush and snow and sleet?
Then try this dandy calendar treat!

It's the scientific sunshine pill
without that bitter, winter chill.

It's mild, relaxing, naturally grown,
it's something that you'll want to own.

It comes in the handy three-month pack:
March, April, May—or your money back.

You'll like its longer, lighter ways,
you'll loiter, linger through its days.

So ask for S-P-R-I-N
G, you'll never regret it;
remember the name,
it's headed for fame,
be the first on your block to get it!

Lights in the Dark

In the quiet
of the night,
shining,
shining,
shining bright.

Emerald stars
or fireflies?

Cat's eyes,
cat's eyes,
cat's eyes.